STEP INTO NATURE

By the Sea

Written by Michael Chinery
Illustrated by John Gosler

GRANADA

Published by Granada Publishing 1984
Granada Publishing Limited
8 Grafton Street, London W1X 3LA

Copyright © Templar Publishing Ltd 1984
Illustrations copyright © Templar Publishing Ltd 1984

British Library Cataloguing in Publication Data
Chinery, Michael
    By the sea.– (Step into Nature; 3)
    1. Seashore biology – juvenile literature
    I. Title   II. Series
    574.909'46   QH95.7

ISBN 0-246-12174-2

Series devised by Richard Carlisle
Edited by Mandy Wood
Designed by Mick McCarthy
Printed in Italy

Contents

No matter where you live, you are surrounded by nature.
In the towns, even in the cities, you will find birds and animals,
plants and trees, and insects to watch and wonder about.
STEP INTO NATURE is about all these things-the everyday
creatures as well as the elusive. It's packed with nature projects
to do, nature diaries to keep and clues and signs for the
nature detective to read. It will teach you how to look at the
world of nature around you, how to understand its working and
how to conserve it for others.

Looking at the seashore

Where the sea meets the land you will find the seashore – a very special kind of habitat where lots of weird and wonderful creatures spend their lives.

Rocky shores occur where the land next to the sea is made of very hard stone. The beach is often covered with boulders and sometimes the land is so hard that it sticks out into the sea to form headlands. Softer rocks are more easily worn away by the waves, to create sandy beaches and sheltered bays.

Apart from rocky and sandy shores, you might also find areas near the coast that are covered in mud. They tend to occur where rivers drain into the sea, bringing with them lots of fine mud and silt. Where areas of mud like this are covered only by the highest tides, salt-marshes develop. They support many grasses and flowers that can survive in this salty environment.

In fact, each different kind of seashore has its own special collection of wildlife. On rocky shores you'll probably find lots and lots of seaweed. It makes an ideal home for crabs, sea snails and all sorts of other tiny creatures. There will also be rock pools to explore – miniature aquariums housing shrimps, sea anemones and others left behind by the receding tide. Sandy shores, on the other hand, look rather lifeless when the tide goes out, but there are actually huge numbers of animals hiding under the sand. There will also be lots of debris washed up on the shore for you to examine.

Pretty pebbles

Pebbles are really bits of rock that have been smoothed by being rolled about by waves. Those from the top of a stony beach are larger than those from the bottom. That's because strong waves throw all sizes of pebbles up onto the shore, but the back-wash can only pull the smaller ones down again.

All legs and beak

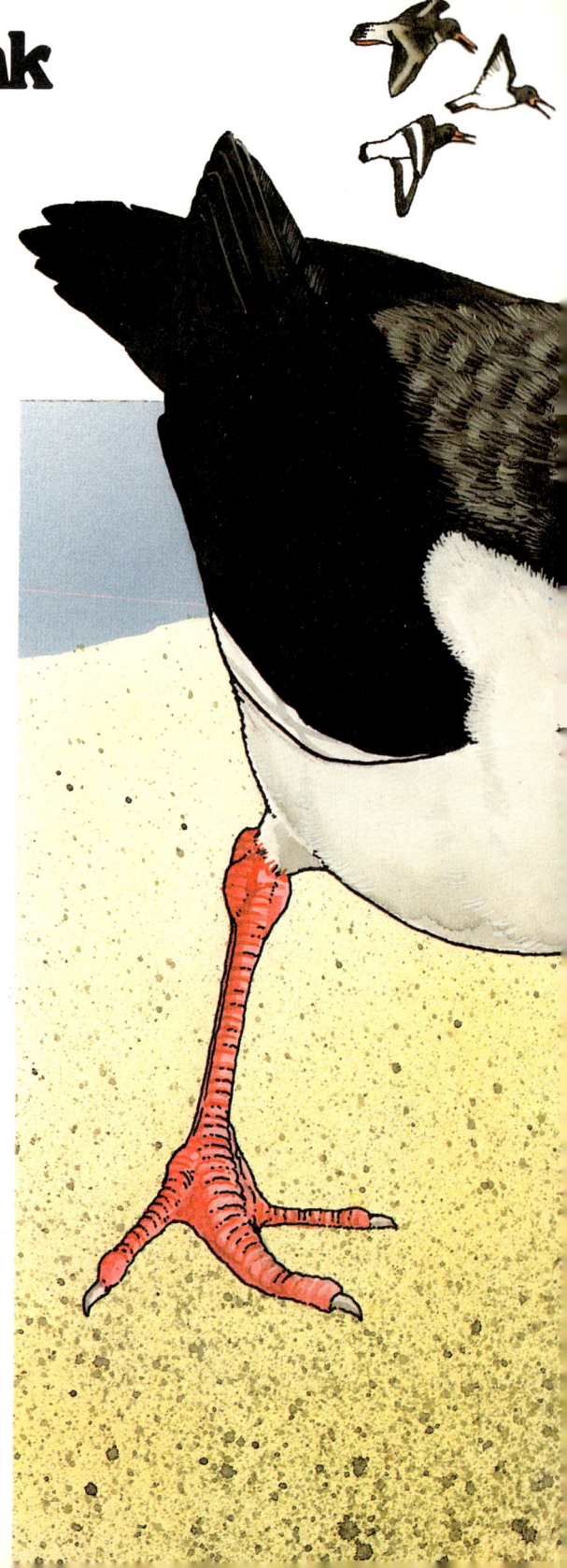

The bird in the big picture is called an oystercatcher. This isn't a very good name for it, though, because it doesn't really catch oysters. Instead, its favourite food is the cockle, which lives under the sand in countless millions. You can often see flocks of oystercatchers working their way along the shore and flicking the cockles out of the sand with their beaks. Once they've done this, they cleverly lever them open with the tip of their beak and scoop out the juicy flesh inside.

You can watch the oystercatcher at work by using your binoculars. But don't go too close or you'll frighten the birds and they'll fly away, making their shrill *cleep-cleep-cleep* alarm call to warn others of the danger. You can also walk along the shore and try counting the empty cockle shells to get an idea of how much the birds eat.

Oystercatchers belong to a group of birds called *waders*. They all have long legs so they can feed in mud and shallow water without spoiling their feathers. Most of them also have long beaks which they dig into the mud in search of food. Many waders breed by inland lakes and marshes in summer and come to the seashore for the winter. Others, like the oystercatcher, stay by the sea throughout the year. How many kinds of waders can you see with your binoculars? Try to see how each kind feeds. Some run about right at the water's edge, looking for food brought in by each wave. Others have special beaks to help them in their search for food. The turnstone, for example, is a fairly small wader that uses its up-turned beak to turn over stones and seaweed, looking for tasty morsels to eat.

Wading in the mud

Try to visit some of the wilder parts of the coast to see wading birds. Take your binoculars and a guide book to help you identify them.

The **avocet** *(left)* sweeps its beak from side to side through shallow water in its search for food. It prefers salt-marshes to open seashores but, on the whole, is rare in Britain.

The **ringed plover** *(right)* is one of the commonest seashore waders. Watch it scuttle along the strand line, stopping here and there to pick up a tasty tit-bit. It nests on stony shores, where its eggs match the stones perfectly.

The **redshank** *(left)* can be distinguished from most other waders by its red legs. When alarmed, it flies away with loud cries of *duke-duke-duke*. It likes muddy shores and salt-marshes.

Catch a crab

Crabs are very common on the shore, but they are not always easy to see. They hide away under the sand or beneath the rocks and seaweeds when the tide goes out, waiting patiently for it to return. You might find a shore crab, like the one in the big picture, lurking among the rock pools high up on the shore. Be careful of the pincers, though, for they can give you a painful nip. One of the best ways to catch this crab is to tie a small piece of meat to some string and dangle it in a likely-looking pool. The crab will probably try to grab the meat with one of its large pincers, and you can then haul it out of the water and have a closer look. Notice the eyes on little stalks, the very hard body covering, and the four pairs of walking legs that the crab has in addition to its pincers.

Most crabs can swim to some extent, but they spend much of their time scuttling about on the sea bed with a strange side-ways motion. Some are true swimmers, and you can recognise them by their hind legs which form broad, flat paddles. One such crab is the velvet or swimming crab which you can see in the circle.

Crabs are scavengers and will eat almost anything. Large ones feed mainly on other animals, both living and dead, which they tear to pieces with their pincers. Smaller crabs generally live by picking up scraps from the sea bed.

Dead crabs are commonly washed up on the beach, but quite often what looks like a crab is just an empty skin. This happens because the crabs have to change their skins several times during their lives. Their hard covering does not allow them to grow in the way that we do, so every now and then they have to get rid of the old coat and grow a larger one.

nature watch

The hermit crab

If you see what you think is a whelk or winkle shell scurrying quickly across the bottom of a rock pool, you can be quite sure that the shell *does not* contain a whelk or a winkle at all, for they are very slow-moving animals. Instead, it is highly likely that the shell contains a hermit crab. This is a very unusual kind of crab which protects its soft, tapering body by living in an empty shell, which it carries about on its back. The shell, of course, doesn't grow along with the crab, so every now and then the hermit crab has to find a bigger one in which to make its new home.

Above: The hermit crab out of its shell, showing the soft, pink body permanently curled to fit the shape of its second-hand home.

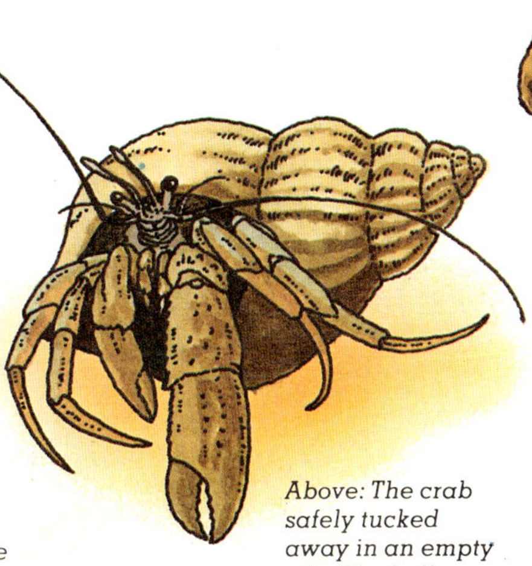

Above: The crab safely tucked away in an empty whelk's shell.

Snails at the seaside

The seaweeds that cover the rocks on the shore provide food and shelter for lots of different animals. But by far the most obvious are the sea snails. If you turn over the seaweeds at low tide you will find all sorts of different kinds lurking under nearly every piece. They are waiting for the tide to return so they can continue their search for food, scraping the seaweeds with their sand-papery tongues.

Not all sea snails live on the rocks, though, and not all of them are vegetarians. Many live in the sand and feed on other animals. In fact, some actually use their tongues like drills to make holes in the shells of cockles and other bivalves so that they can scrape out the soft flesh inside.

Next time you're on the beach, try collecting as many different empty shells as you can. You may find that some of the bivalve shells washed up on the beach will have a neat hole in them drilled by one of the flesh-eating snails.

The flesh-eating snails also eat dead animals and help to keep the sea bed clean. You can see them in action if you find a dead crab or other animal on the beach. Tie it to a long piece of string or a fishing line and throw it out into the water. If you pull it gently in after a few minutes you might well find several whelks or dog whelks feeding on it. You can also try this experiment with a piece of meat or fish.

On the right you can see the shells of some common sea snails. Notice the different ways that their shells coil. Make a permanent collection of empty shells from the beach and try to name them all with the help of a guide book. (You can see some bivalve shells on page 28.)

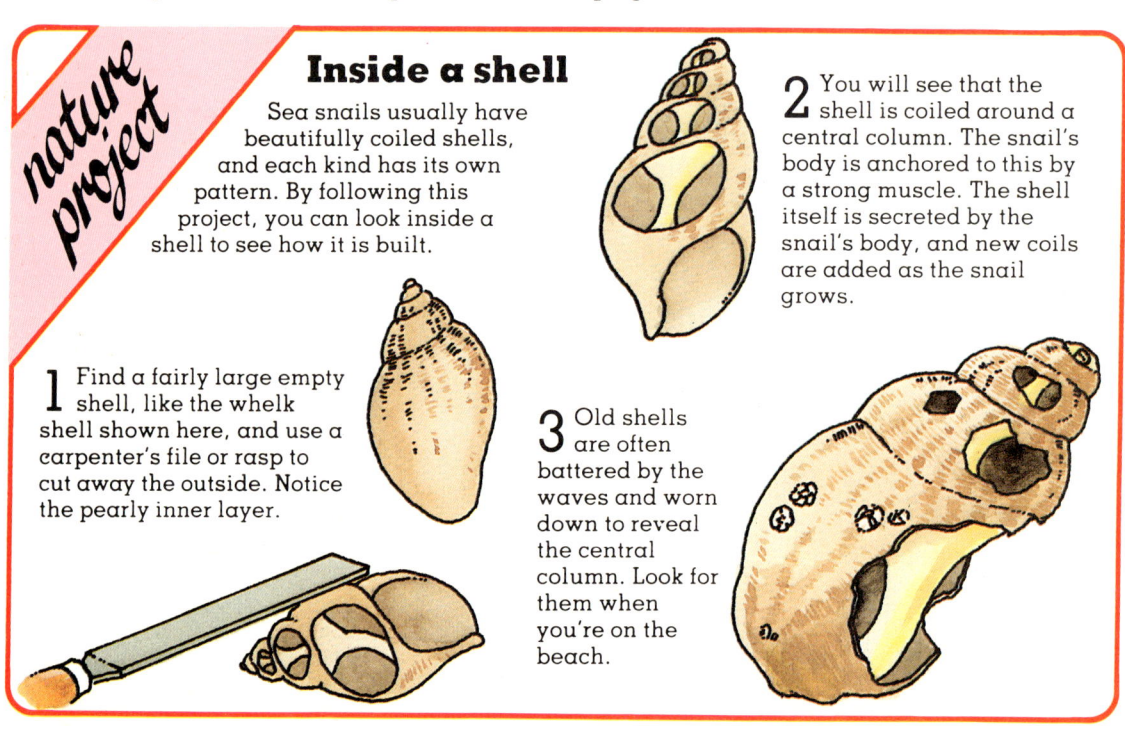

nature project

Inside a shell

Sea snails usually have beautifully coiled shells, and each kind has its own pattern. By following this project, you can look inside a shell to see how it is built.

2 You will see that the shell is coiled around a central column. The snail's body is anchored to this by a strong muscle. The shell itself is secreted by the snail's body, and new coils are added as the snail grows.

1 Find a fairly large empty shell, like the whelk shell shown here, and use a carpenter's file or rasp to cut away the outside. Notice the pearly inner layer.

3 Old shells are often battered by the waves and worn down to reveal the central column. Look for them when you're on the beach.

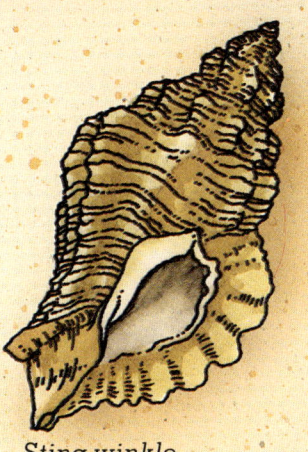

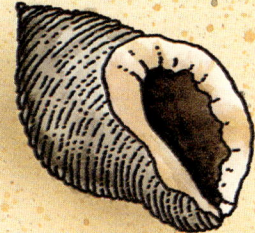

Common dog whelk
All kinds of shores: feeds on other animals. Up to 4.5cms high.

Sting winkle
All kinds of shores: drills into other shells. Up to 6cms high.

Painted topshell
Rocky shores: feeds on seaweeds. Up to 2.5cms high.

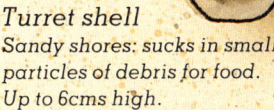

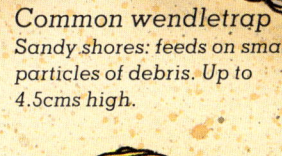

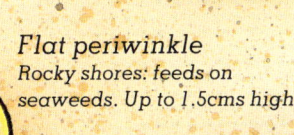

Turret shell
Sandy shores: sucks in small particles of debris for food. Up to 6cms high.

Common wendletrap
Sandy shores: feeds on small particles of debris. Up to 4.5cms high.

Flat periwinkle
Rocky shores: feeds on seaweeds. Up to 1.5cms high.

Pelican's-foot shell
Sandy shores, rarely above low-water mark. Feeds on particles of debris. Up to 5cms high.

Common periwinkle
Rocky shores: feeds on seaweeds. Up to 2.5cms high. This is the fishmonger's winkle.

Common necklace shell
Sandy shores: bores into bivalves. Up to 2cms high.

Blue-rayed limpet
Rocky shores: feeds on seaweeds. Up to 2cms long.

Ormer
Rocky shores in warmer areas: feeds on seaweeds. Up to 8cms long.

Common cowrie
Rocky shores: feeds on seasquirts. Up to 1.5cms long.

11

All arms and no head

The orangey-red creature in the big picture is called a sunstar, and it's just one of the many different kinds of starfish that live in the sea all over the world. Look out for them in rock pools or among the stones and seaweeds at around low tide level. If you find one, run your fingers gently over its surface and you will find it is very rough. These animals belong to a group known as *echinoderms*, which means "spiny skins". Sea urchins (see page 30) also belong to this group.

Starfish have no head and no eyes. In fact, they don't even have a real brain. And their mouth is underneath their body, right in the centre. One thing that the starfish does have plenty of, though, is arms. Most starfish have five arms, but the sunstar has up to thirteen! If you look at the underside of these arms, you will see hundreds of tiny tubes. They are called tube feet and each one is full of water. At the end of every foot there is a tiny suction pad, and the starfish uses these to pull itself along. Although each pad is very small, there are so many of them that their combined pull is very powerful. Some starfish even use them to open cockles and other shellfish – by wrapping its arms around a shell and applying the tube-feet, the starfish can pull the two halves of the shell apart to get at its meal inside.

The other animal in the big picture is called a brittle star. It is related to the starfish but its arms are much more slender and sharply separated from each other. The arms break very easily, and this is how the animal gets its name. There are many different kinds of brittle star – you might find some crawling around low tide level, but many others hide away in the sand.

Growing new arms

Starfish have an amazing ability to repair themselves. If one of their arms is snapped off, they simply grow a replacement. The starfish below is doing just that – you can see that the new arm is shorter than all the rest. It will take several months to reach full size. A torn-off arm can even grow a new body, so you might even find a starfish with one large arm and four tiny ones!

Turn over please!

Find a live starfish in the shallows and turn it on its back. Watch the tiny tube-feet waving about. Eventually they will get a hold on a stone or some seaweed and will gradually haul the whole animal the right way up again.

13

Exploring rock pools

Even the hardest rocks on the shore end up being worn away by the water and stones that are thrown at them by every wave. But the softest or weakest parts are the first to be broken down, leaving behind hollows of various shapes and sizes in the rocks. These hollows hold back some of the sea water when the tide goes out, forming the familiar pools that you'll find on any rocky beach. They're really nature's very own aquaria in which you can watch a wide variety of animals as they carry on with their lives, just as if the tide were still in. Remember to be very careful when exploring these pools, though, because some of the rocks surrounding them can be very sharp.

And, if they are covered with seaweed, they can also be very slippery. Wear plimsolls or similar shoes with a good grip to prevent you falling over.

The big picture below shows some of the things that you might find in such a pool. First of all, there are the seaweeds. The two brown ones are called toothed wrack, on the left, and bladder wrack, on the right. You will often find green and red seaweed in the pools as well, and the bottom may be coloured pink by some very unusual red seaweed which forms hard crusts on the rocks. In the middle of the picture there is something that looks a lot like a plant but, in fact, is really a very simple kind

of animal. It's called a breadcrumb sponge and it is one of the permanent pool-dwellers, fixed to the rocks for all of its life. It ranges from white to green or brown in colour. It feeds by filtering minute particles from the water.

The big animal in the middle of the picture is a common prawn. The prawns you normally see will be cooked and pink in colour. But when they are alive they are almost transparent and very difficult to see. Another prawn, called the chameleon prawn, can actually change its colour to match different backgrounds. It is green when amongst green seaweed, but if you put it with brown seaweed it will turn brown.

There are three other creatures living in the pool as well. They are all mentioned elsewhere in this book. Can you name them?

nature project

Looking underwater

It is not always easy to see into a rock pool, especially if the sun is shining overhead. But there are several different ways of solving the problem. You could, for instance, wear a diver's mask and lower your head so that the mask is just under the surface. Another way is to cut the bottom out of an old plastic bucket and replace it with a sheet of clear

 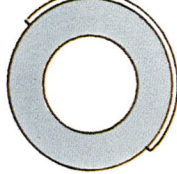

plastic. (In fact, a sheet of clear polythene held on by string or elastic bands will do.) You can then lower the bucket into the water and you will be able to see what is going on underneath quite clearly. If you can't use either of these methods, get someone to hold a sunshade or umbrella over the pool to keep the sun off while you study the watery depths!

nature detective

Shrimp or prawn?

If your rock pool has a sandy bottom it may contain shrimps as well as prawns, although shrimps usually prefer sandy seashores. You can tell the two apart if you look closely because prawns are larger than shrimps and have a toothed spine on the top of their head.

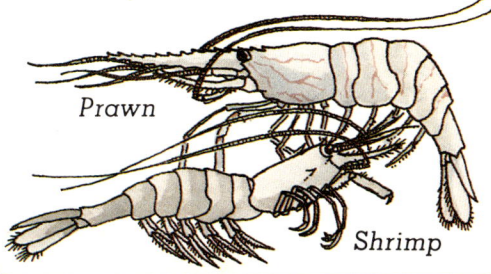

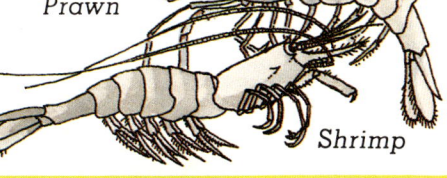

Prawn

Shrimp

An expert swimmer

Have you ever seen a seal? These animals spend most of their time in the sea, but you can sometimes see them basking on the shore at low tide. You will have to go to some of the wilder parts of the coast to see them, and you will need some binoculars if you want to get a really good view.

Two kinds of seal live around the coasts of Britain. The one in the big picture is the common seal. It has a rather short muzzle, slightly hollow on the top, and its nostrils form a distinct "V" shape. It likes sheltered bays and estuaries and doesn't go far out to sea. The grey seal, which can be grey or brown, has a much longer and flatter muzzle, as you can see in the small picture. Its nostrils do not form a "V". The grey seal prefers rockier and more exposed coastlines.

Seals are flesh-eating mammals like dogs and cats. Long ago, the seals' ancestors lived on land just like these other animals, but then they began to hunt in the water for food. They found lots of tasty fish there and soon began to spend more and more time swimming in the water instead of walking around on land. Their bodies gradually changed to help them in their new surroundings and, consequently, today's seals are

Grey seal

wonderfully built for swimming. Their legs have turned into flippers and their bodies are beautifully streamlined to help them glide smoothly through the water. The hind flippers are held close together and move from side to side like a fish's tail to push the seal through the water. The front flippers are used for steering. Seals can hunt fish under water for as long as 30 minutes at a time, but they have to surface regularly in order to breathe. They spend most of their time swimming gracefully about in the water but they have to come onto land to have their babies. Without proper legs, they are rather clumsy when out of the water and can only wriggle about on the beach.

If you look at the hind flippers of the common seal in the picture you will see a plastic clip. Biologists used to put these on baby seals to try to find out how long they lived and how far they travelled. You might, very occasionally, find one of these clips washed up on the beach.

If you have been to a zoo or a circus you will probably have seen the seals' cousins, the sea lions. These usually come from California and they differ from the true seals in several ways. They have much bigger flippers and they can waddle along on them quite rapidly. The sea lions also have ear flaps, which you will not find on ordinary seals. Try to find some pictures of sea lions and spot these differences yourself.

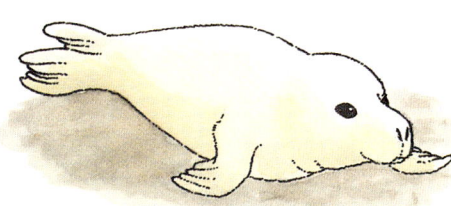

nature watch

Growing up in the cold

Seals live mainly in cold areas and, as well as nice fur coats, they also have a thick layer of fat just underneath the skin. This fat is called blubber and it helps to keep the seals warm. The pups don't have much of this fat when they are born, but their mothers feed them with

rich milk and they soon fatten up. They all have fur coats when they are born, though. Common seal pups are born in summer and are brown. They can swim straight away. Grey seal pups (like the one above) are born in the autumn. They are white at birth and stay white for several weeks. They do not go into the water until they are about three weeks old.

Greedy gulls

It's not often that you visit the seaside without seeing some seagulls gliding lazily overhead. They don't make much noise when they're in the air, but if you throw some food down for them they will swoop to the ground and squabble noisily over it. Gulls are scavengers and they will eat almost anything that they can find. On the shore, they search the strand line for living and dead animal matter, and also probe the mud and sand to find worms and other creatures to eat. They'll even follow ships out to sea and feast on the kitchen scraps that are thrown overboard. They may drop down and snatch the food from the water, or else settle on the surface to feed like ducks. Many gulls also fly far inland, especially in the winter, to feed on rubbish dumps and farmland.

One of the commonest gulls is the herring gull, which you can see in the big picture. It is about 60 cms long – roughly the same size as a farmyard duck – and it usually has pink legs, although birds living around the Mediterranean have yellow legs. There is also a lesser black-backed gull in the picture. You will often find this bird with the herring gulls. It is about the same size but it has a darker back and wings and always has yellow legs. Both gulls make their nests among cliff-top grasses, on sand dunes, or on cliff-ledges. The herring gull also nests on town buildings and is so common in some towns that it has become a real pest. Its droppings make a mess and its nest, which is made from piles of grass and seaweed, is usually very smelly.

The gulls won't usually let you get too close to them, so use your binoculars to get a better view.

Gulls overhead

Use your binoculars and a good bird guide to see how many different kinds of bird you can find at the seaside. Not all of them are gulls. You can see some more seabirds on pages 6, 34 and 40.

Winter

Summer

The **black-headed gull** (*above*) is the commonest gull in most parts of Europe – inland as well as by the sea. It has a black head only in the summer.

The **common tern** (*left*) is related to the gulls but has a narrower beak and a forked tail. It hovers over the waves and plunges down to catch fish.

The **fulmar** (*right*) is not a gull. Look at the beak and you will see that it has tubular nostrils.

The **kittiwake** (*left*) is a true gull, with black legs and black wing-tips. It nests on cliff ledges.

Flowers of the seashore

Next time you're at the seaside you might notice that very few flowers grow in the sea itself. However, there are plenty to be found growing on the upper part of the shore, just out of reach of the waves. They are all rather special plants which don't mind the salty spray that covers them every day. Most ordinary plants are killed by salt, but those that live on the shore have adapted to cope with their harsh life.

You will find that the plants growing on muddy shores are quite different from those on sandy beaches and shingle. Plants growing on shingle usually have *very* long roots. This is because the upper layers of shingle are very dry and the long roots are necessary to reach the water far below the surface. Plants growing on sand generally have long underground stems that creep horizontally through the ground. They help to bind together the loose sand and stop it from blowing around too much. When the sand has been anchored like this many other plants can also grow. On page 32 you can read about some of the plants that grow on cliffs.

Up to 120cms

Up to 100cms

Up to 40cms

Up to 120cms

Sea beet is a straggly plant which grows well on shingle and is very common on sea walls along wild parts of the coast.

Sea purslane can be easily identified by its grey leaves. It grows in damper parts of salt-marshes and is frequently covered by the tide.

Sea lavender grows well on salt-marshes. Its broad, flat flower heads turn the marshes pale mauve in July and August.

Marram grass has creeping underground stems and stiff leaves that play an important part in anchoring shifting sand dunes.

Up to 90cms

Sea pea has thick, fleshy stems which creep over shingle beaches. Its flowers can be found at most times of the year.

Up to 60cms

Sea bindweed generally creeps over sand dunes, where its beautiful flowers can be seen from June to September.

Up to 60cms

Sea holly, named after its very prickly leaves, grows on both sand and shingle. It flowers from June to September.

Up to 20cms

Sea sandwort has very thick leaves which form bright green carpets on the shingle. The tiny greenish flowers appear in summer.

Up to 80cms

Yellow horned-poppy gets its name from its seed pods which are like long horns. It grows on shingle and flowers in summer.

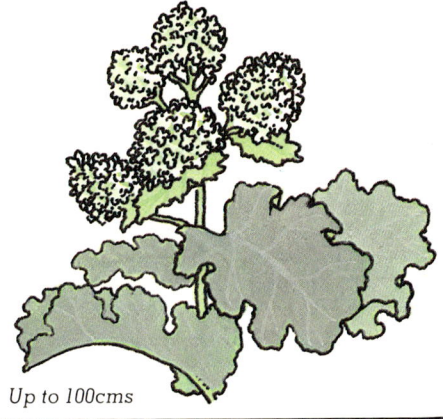

Up to 100cms

Sea kale grows in very large clumps, mainly on shingle, and flowers in June. Its leaves are like those of a large cabbage.

Stranded by the sea

Twice in every 24 hours the tide sweeps in over the seashore and covers the sand and rocks. Each wave breaks slightly further up the shore than the previous one, until the water reaches high tide level. Then the tide turns and starts to go slowly out again.

Just over six hours later, the water will be lapping several metres down-shore around the low water mark. Then the tide will turn again and start to creep back up the beach as it has done for millions upon millions of years. The incoming tide is called the *flow tide* and the out-going tide is the *ebb tide*.

Exact tide levels vary from day to day. Once a month we get very high tides called *spring tides*. During the two weeks after these spring tides, the high water mark gets lower each day. It then

starts to move up the beach again until we get the next spring tides. Try to find out what causes the tide to ebb and flow. You will probably be surprised to learn that the sun and the moon are involved.

As the waves sweep in over the beach, they bring with them all kinds of rubbish. This debris is gradually pushed further and further up the shore until it is left in a line along the high water mark. This is called the strand line. Have a good look along it when you next visit the seaside. You will find lots of interesting things there, some of which you can see in the big picture. You might even find several strand lines during the days after a spring tide, because the high water mark gets lower

1. Cork float
2. Old bottle
3. "Mermaid's purse" – the egg case of a dog fish
4. Dead crab
5. Seagull skull
6. Mussel shell
7. Whelk shell
8. Cockle shell
9. Gribble
10. Bird ring
11. Sea urchin shell
12. Driftwood
13. Old rope
14. Dead starfish
15. Crab pincer
16. Glass float from a fishing net
17. Sea urchin shell
18. Topshell
19. Cuttlebone – the skeleton of a cuttlefish

each day. Use your diary to note the time of the high tide each day. Is it always at the same time?

Seaweeds make up the bulk of the strand line, but you will also find lots of driftwood there – some of it washed overboard from ships and some of it, in the form of roots and branches, brought down to the sea by rivers or by cliff ledges collapsing. Often the wood takes on fascinating shapes – you might even like to take some bits home with you for ornaments. If you look at a piece of driftwood closely, you may well find that it is riddled with holes. See if you can find any of the tiny creatures that made them: one of the commonest is a little woodlouse-like creature called a gribble.

Empty sea shells and dead animals, like crabs and starfishes, are also common on the strand line, and so, unfortunately, are glass and plastic bottles. If you turn over some of this debris you will find lots of small animals hiding underneath, including sand-hoppers which leap all over the place. These animals feed on the debris and gradually help to get rid of it. Unfortunately, though, they cannot destroy the man-made plastic and other rubbish that is left behind by careless people. So always make sure that you take *all* your litter with you when you leave the beach.

Plant or animal?

The sea anemone looks like a flower and is even named after one. It has colourful "petals" and it stays in one place just like a plant. In fact, many people think it *is* a plant, but the sea anemone is really a flesh-eating animal. And its "petals" are really poisonous tentacles with which it catches fish and other small water creatures.

Some sea anemones anchor themselves in the sand, but most kinds fix themselves to the rocks instead. You can often find them in rock pools, and although they look permanently fixed they can actually glide very slowly over the rocks to find a new home. If you make a mark on the rock surface close to an anemone and then look at it every day, you might even be able to find out how far an anemone can move.

Many anemones are uncovered when the tide goes out, but they don't mind this as long as they are not in the full sun. They merely pull their tentacles right inside their bodies and wait like little blobs of jelly for the tide to return.

When they are covered by water again, they put out their tentacles and wait for some food to come floating along. Then, when a fish or other small animal brushes past, the tentacles fire out hundreds of minute, poisonous darts which are attached to the anemone by tiny threads. The fish is thus trapped by the tiny darts sticking into it, and quickly becomes paralysed by the poison. Once the anemone is sure of its catch, it uses its tentacles to push the fish into its mouth. Each poison dart can be used only once and then the anemone gets rid of it, but all the time the tentacles are making more. For this reason, you shouldn't touch sea anemones. Not all of them can hurt you, but some of the larger ones can give a nasty sting.

Sea anemones have no skeleton at all, but their close relatives the corals form hard cups of limestone around themselves. In warm seas these corals build up huge colonies called *reefs*.

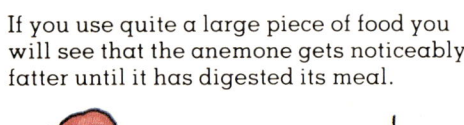

nature watch

Feeding anemones

It is very easy to watch the feeding action of the sea anemone's tentacles. All you need is a small piece of meat or fish – some scraps left over from your lunch will be fine. Tie the food to a piece of string or cotton and then look for an anemone with its tentacles open in a rock pool. Dangle the food in the tentacles and watch what happens. You will not be able to see the poison darts shoot out because they are far too small, but you will see the tentacles clinging to the food and gradually bending over to push it into the mouth. The mouth is right in the centre of the ring of tentacles.

If you use quite a large piece of food you will see that the anemone gets noticeably fatter until it has digested its meal.

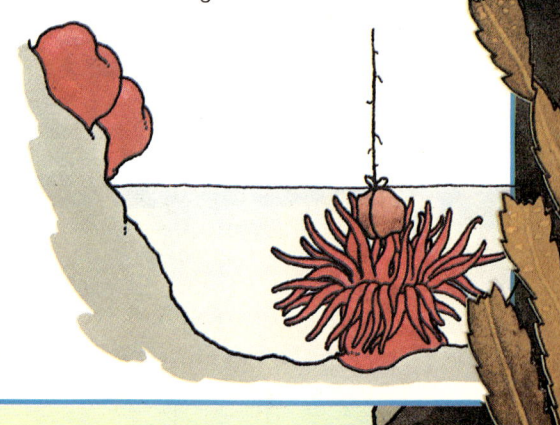

Beach invaders

Jellyfish are close relatives of sea anemones, but they float freely around in the sea instead of being anchored to the rocks or sand. Some have tentacles 30 metres long and are dangerous to people because of their stings.

Others have very short tentacles and no stings: they feed by sucking in tiny animals from the water. Jellyfish are often washed up on the beach where they quickly die. The **common jellyfish** (*below left*) is harmless, but the **Portuguese man-of-war** (*below*) has a very dangerous sting. Do not touch it.

Seaweed everywhere

Seaweeds are rather simple plants – they don't have any flowers and they don't have any real roots either. Instead, they are just made up of one or more leafy fronds, sometimes with stalks attached. Seaweeds belong to the group of plants called *algae* and there are about 1000 different kinds growing around the coasts of Europe. They can be split up into three main types – green, brown, and red.

Some seaweeds, mainly red and brown kinds, form dense beds on stones and mud just below the low tide level, but many others grow all over the beach, in places where they are sometimes left uncovered when the tide goes out. Have a good look at a seaweed-covered beach – rocky shores are particularly good for this – and you will see that the weeds are not scattered about haphazardly. They grow in definite zones.

Right at the top of the shore there is often a zone of the brown seaweed called *channelled wrack*. Its fronds are quite narrow and have a groove along their centre. These grooves trap the sea water and prevent the plant from drying out, for there are often days when the tide

does not cover the channelled wrack at all. The green, tubular fronds of *sea grass (Enteromorpha)* are often mingled with the channelled wrack, especially in and around pools and wherever fresh water runs over the rocks. You may also find the broad fronds of *sea lettuce* growing in the same place.

Twisted wrack, with its spirally twisted fronds, grows further down the beach in a zone just below the channelled wrack. Then come the various other brown seaweeds, including *bladder wrack* and *toothed wrack*. The red seaweeds, such as *laver* and *carragheen* (sometimes called Irish moss), grow mainly on the lower parts of the shore. The seaweeds are zoned in this way because each kind can only stand being out of the water for so long. Which kinds do you think can stand the *least* exposure to the air? Mark each zone as it is uncovered by the tide. How long before the tide covers each zone again?

① *Channelled wrack*
② *Sea grass*
③ *Sea lettuce*
④ *Twisted wrack*
⑤ *Toothed wrack*
⑥ *Carragheen*
⑦ *Laver*

Which weed is which?

The colour and shape of a seaweed's fronds are the main things to look at when trying to identify it. See how many different kinds you can find. Some of the commonest are illustrated below.

Bladder wrack *(right)* is also known as pop-weed because of the air-filled bladders that cover its fronds. Try popping them with your fingers. They help to buoy up the fronds in the water.

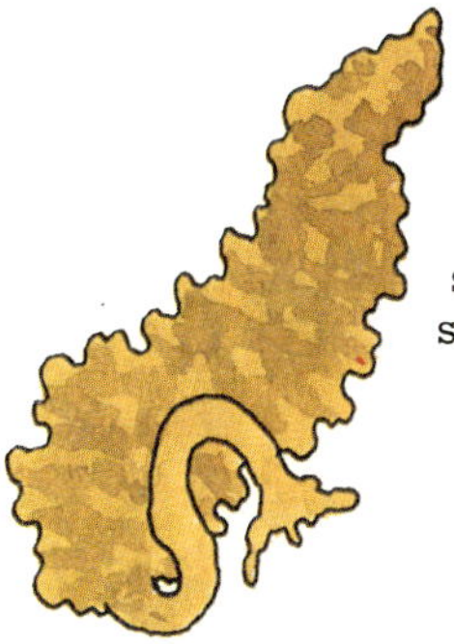

Sea belt *(left)*, also known as oarweed, is one of the largest seaweeds – its fronds sometimes growing to 9 metres in length. It grows on the lower half of the shore.

Dulse *(right)* is a common red seaweed. Its fronds are roughly fan-shaped, often with smaller fans growing from the edges. It usually grows low down on the shore, often on large brown seaweeds.

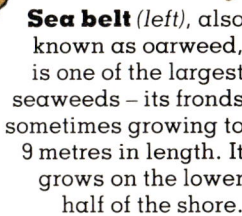

Coral weed *(left)* is a rather stiff red seaweed, found on the lower shore and in rock pools. It is coated with a hard chalky crust. Up to 15cms long, it is pink or purple but becomes white when it dies.

Hiding in the sand

You will not see much animal life on a sandy beach at low tide, but if you had X-ray eyes and could look right down into the sand, it would be quite a different matter. For living beneath the beach, you would see millions of small creatures, including many kinds of worms and sea snails. But the best known of all the sand dwellers are the bivalves. These are soft-bodied animals with two shells hinged along one edge.

The shells of dead bivalves are very common on the shore. You might be lucky enough to find a complete one, but the hinge usually breaks after a while so most of the shells that you see lying on the sand will be single ones. Look at the inside and you will see two scars, showing where the powerful shell-closing muscles were once fixed.

To find living bivalves, you will normally have to dig down into the sand – and dig quite quickly. Bivalves don't look very active, but some can burrow quite fast when they have to, using a very muscular part of their bodies called the *foot*. The bivalve uses it to dig and to drag its body down into the sand. In fact, the razor shell on the left of the picture is said to be able to burrow faster than a man can dig!

When the tide is in, the bivalves open their shells and push two tubes, called *siphons*, up to the surface to feed. Water is drawn in through one tube, and minute food particles – mostly decaying matter – are filtered out before the water is released through the other tube.

Not all bivalves burrow in the sand, though. The piddock actually bores into rocks using its sharp-edged shell and the scallop simply rests on the sea bed, swimming about by flapping its shells.

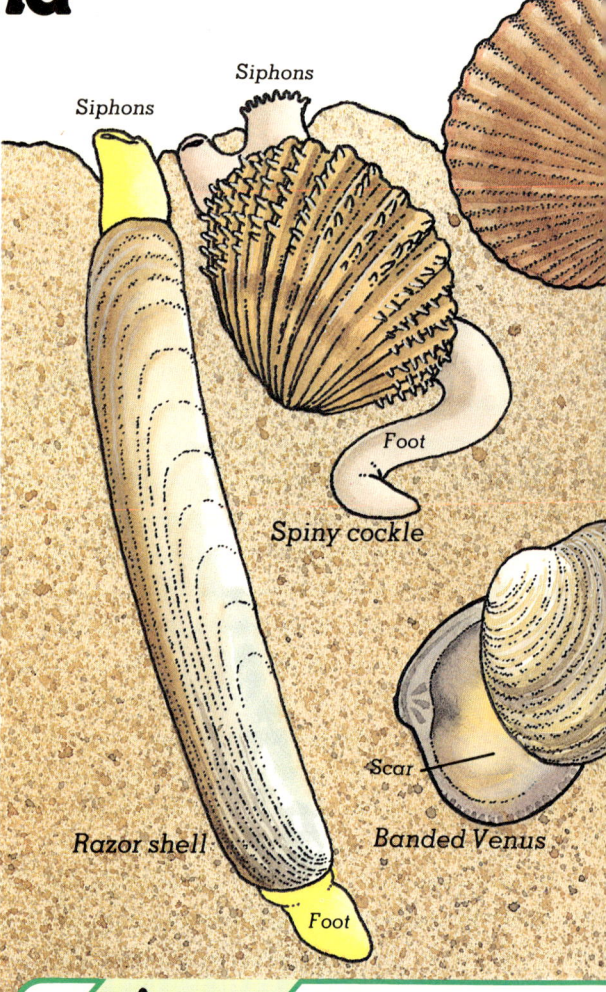

Siphons

Siphons

Siphons

Foot

Spiny cockle

Razor shell

Scar

Banded Venus

Foot

The lugworm's tunnel

Millions of lugworms live in the sand of the seashore. You can find them by looking for tell-tale signs on the surface. Safe in its L-shaped burrow, the worm sucks in sand and digests any plant and animal matter that it finds. Then it pushes out the undigested sand in little mounds on the surface above. These tell you where to dig for the worm. Look out also for the shallow depressions which show where the worm is sucking in sand. Fishermen dig up lots of lugworms for bait!

Siphons

Scallop

Piddock

Gaper

nature project

Feeding shells

Try to dig up some live cockles from a sandy or muddy beach. A local fisherman may help you to find them. You can then see how they feed by setting up this simple experiment. You will need a jam jar half full of the sand or mud in which your cockle was living, some sea water and, of course, a cockle!

1 Top your jar up with sea water, add a cockle and leave for a few hours. The cockle will burrow into the sand and start to feed. Use an eye-dropper to put a few drops of gravy above the cockle's siphons.

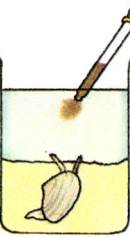

2 If you watch closely you will be able to see the gravy being sucked down through the water and into one of the cockle's siphons.

If you can find the beautiful shell of the tellin while you are digging in the sand you will be able to watch a different kind of feeding activity. The tellin has one very long siphon and one shorter one. Instead of merely sucking up water, the animal uses its long inlet siphon rather like a vacuum cleaner to suck up bits of food from the surface of the sand.

29

Prickly urchins

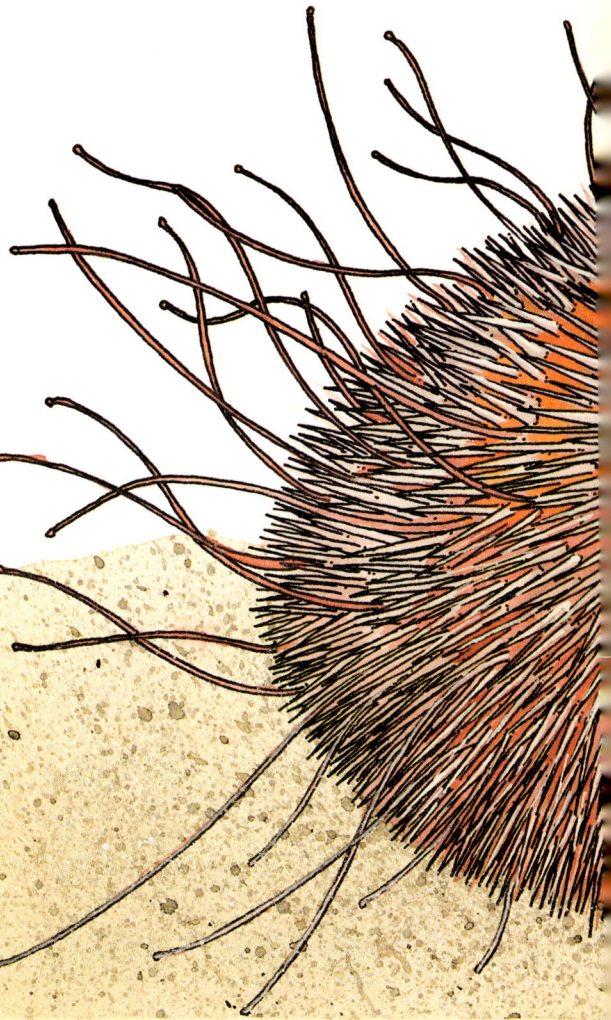

The animal in the big picture is an edible sea urchin. It may not look very edible, but many people like to eat the soft parts in the middle of the prickly body. Our drawing shows what it looks like when alive, but you are much more likely to find its empty, spineless shell washed up on the beach. You can sometimes find living ones, though, if you try hard enough. Look for them among the stones and seaweed around low tide level, especially in rocky areas.

Sea urchins don't look much like starfish but, in fact, they're really quite closely related. Neither creature has a proper front or back. And there is not even a head or a true brain. You can read about starfish on page 12.

The shell of the sea urchin is just underneath its skin and it is made up of lots of chalky plates fused together. It has spines for protection which come from small pimples on the shell, and also lots of things called *tube-feet*. If you examine an empty shell carefully, you will see five double rows of little holes spreading out in lines from the top. The animal's delicate tube-feet stick out through these holes. They are full of water and, apart from helping the animal to move about, they also have suction pads on the ends to anchor the urchin firmly to the rocks. You can see the spines and the tube-feet in the big picture.

There are many different kinds of sea urchin. Most of them are bun-shaped, with a domed top and a flat bottom, and they live among the stones and seaweeds just like the edible urchin. They feed mainly on seaweeds, which they scrape and chew with their powerful teeth. (You can see the urchin's mouth in the picture, in the centre of its underside.)

However, there are other urchins that live in the sand on the sea bed and feed on tiny particles of plant and animal matter. Some of their tube feet are specially modified for digging, while others are very sticky and are used for collecting food particles. These burrowing urchins are commonly heart-shaped and their empty shells are often washed up on the beach. They are very fragile and easily broken.

Be very careful if you go paddling in areas where there are sea urchins, for their sharp spines can inflict very painful wounds. Because of this it's a good idea to wear beach shoes or old plimsolls when you're in the water.

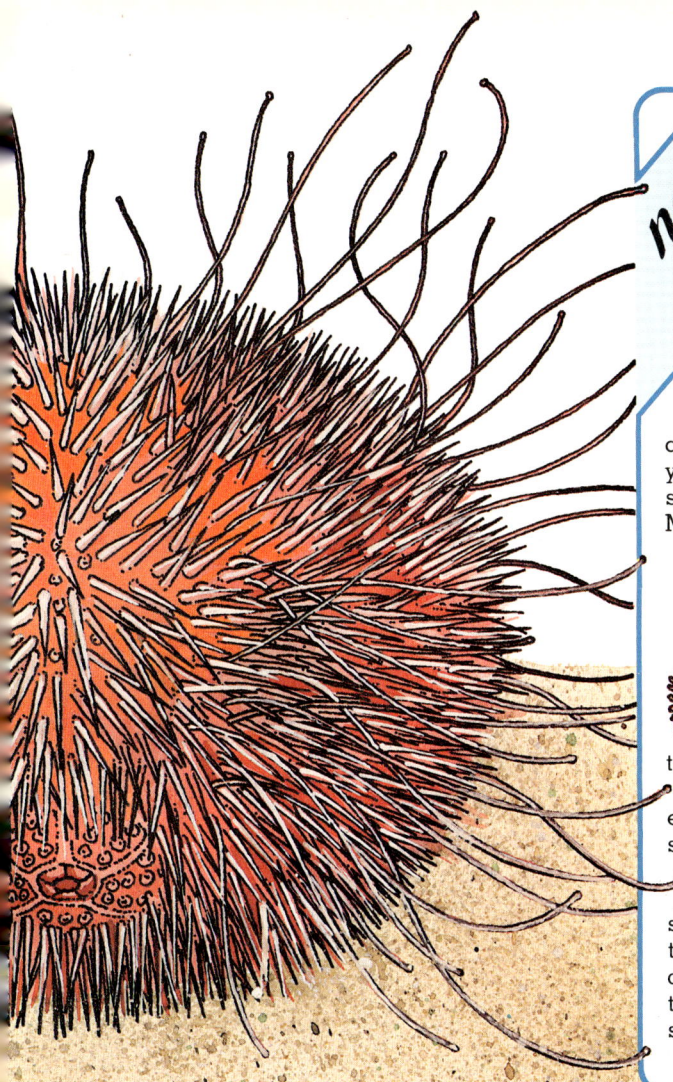

Curious cucumbers

Sea cucumbers are sausage-shaped relatives of the sea urchins, but they have neither spines nor shells. There are many different kinds. Most of them burrow in the sand or mud of the sea bed, often far out to sea, but some can be found on rocky shores. Look for them in pools and narrow crevices. If you pick one up you will find that it has tough, leathery skin and rows of tube-feet on its underside. Most sea cucumbers are also rather sticky

to touch, and if you disturb one it may give you a surprise by squirting water everywhere! At first sight, there doesn't seem to be any front or back to the animal, but if you put it into a bowl of sea water and leave it for a while, you will see some feathery tentacles emerge from the front end. The cucumber uses these to collect food particles from the sea bed – they are really special tube-feet used to shovel food into the animal's mouth.

The urchin's camouflage

The rock urchin lives among rocks, usually quite low down on the shore, and often scrapes a deep hole for itself in which to live. It picks up bits of broken shells and weed with its tube-feet and sticks them onto its body to camouflage itself. If you use some tweezers to pull off the debris, you can then watch the urchin pick them up again. How long does it take to camouflage itself? This urchin is most common around the warmer shores of southern Europe. Look for it on the rocks at low tide.

Flowers on high

Seaside cliffs are often made very colourful in the summer by all the different kinds of flowers that grow on them. Some of the flowers grow on the tops of cliffs and you can easily see them if there is a cliff-top path for you to walk along. Other plants grow on the steep faces of the cliffs themselves and are not so easy to examine. Don't be tempted to climb the cliffs in order to take a look at the plants, though, for they are dangerous places. A far better way of getting a closer look is to use some binoculars.

Cliff faces are very windy places, and the plants growing there have long roots to help anchor them firmly in the cracks and crannies. Many of them also have thick, fleshy leaves which are used to store water. This is very important because cliff faces can become very dry in a hot summer.

Rocky cliffs aren't very different from old walls and rocky roadsides, and several cliff plants also grow in these other places. In fact, the wallflower even got its name because it grows on old walls! Some of the commonest cliff plants are shown here. How many can you find when you are at the seaside?

Spring squill is a seaside cousin of the bluebell. It grows in grassy places, usually on cliff tops, and flowers from April to June.

Hoary stock is rare in the wild in Britain, but common in gardens and elsewhere in Europe. It flowers from May to July.

Wild wallflowers always have yellow or orange flowers, which appear from March until June. They grow in cracks on cliffs and walls.

Thrift, also called sea pink, forms neat cushions on cliff faces and among cliff-top grasses. It flowers all summer.

English stonecrop forms mats on the rocks. Its fleshy leaves are greyish green at first but then turn red. It flowers in summer.

Scurvy grass is not really a grass, but a member of the cabbage family. It grows on salt-marshes and at the bottoms of cliffs.

Buckshorn plantain grows all over the cliffs and also on fixed sand dunes. Its flower spikes appear from May to October.

Hottentot fig is a beautiful plant which originally came from South Africa. It grows on cliffs and dunes. Its flowers are pink or yellow.

Rock samphire grows on sand dunes as well as on cliffs. It has greyish fleshy leaves and it flowers from July to October.

Sea campion grows on the cliff tops and also on shingle beaches, usually forming neat cushions. It flowers all summer.

The comical puffin

The puffin is sometimes called the "clown of birds" because of its huge beak, which looks just like a painted mask. But if you want to see these funny birds, you will have to visit some of the wilder parts of the coast where there are steep cliffs. Remember also to go looking for them only in the spring and summer, for outside their breeding season the puffins move far out to sea.

Puffins usually nest in burrows on grassy cliff-tops. The female lays one white egg and the parents then take turns to sit on it for about six weeks until it hatches. They look after the young puffin for another six weeks and then fly off out to sea, leaving it all alone on the cliff-top. The chick waits for a few days and then waddles to the edge of the cliff. It has never flown or swum before, but still it launches itself fearlessly into the air and glides down to the water.

Although puffins are a bit clumsy on land, they are graceful fliers. But where they really excel themselves is in the water, for they are superb swimmers. They look rather like ducks when swimming on the surface, but when they are hungry they turn into living submarines and chase fish under the water at great speed. They drive themselves along by flapping their wings, just as if they were flying through the sea instead of the air. Their favourite fish are sand-eels, which they catch in great quantities. Toothed ridges inside their beaks enable these birds to hold securely onto a batch of sand-eels while still snapping up more! In fact, puffins have been known to return to their nests with up to thirty sand-eels held in just one beak. Such large numbers are unusual, however, and most birds carry only between five and ten fish at a time.

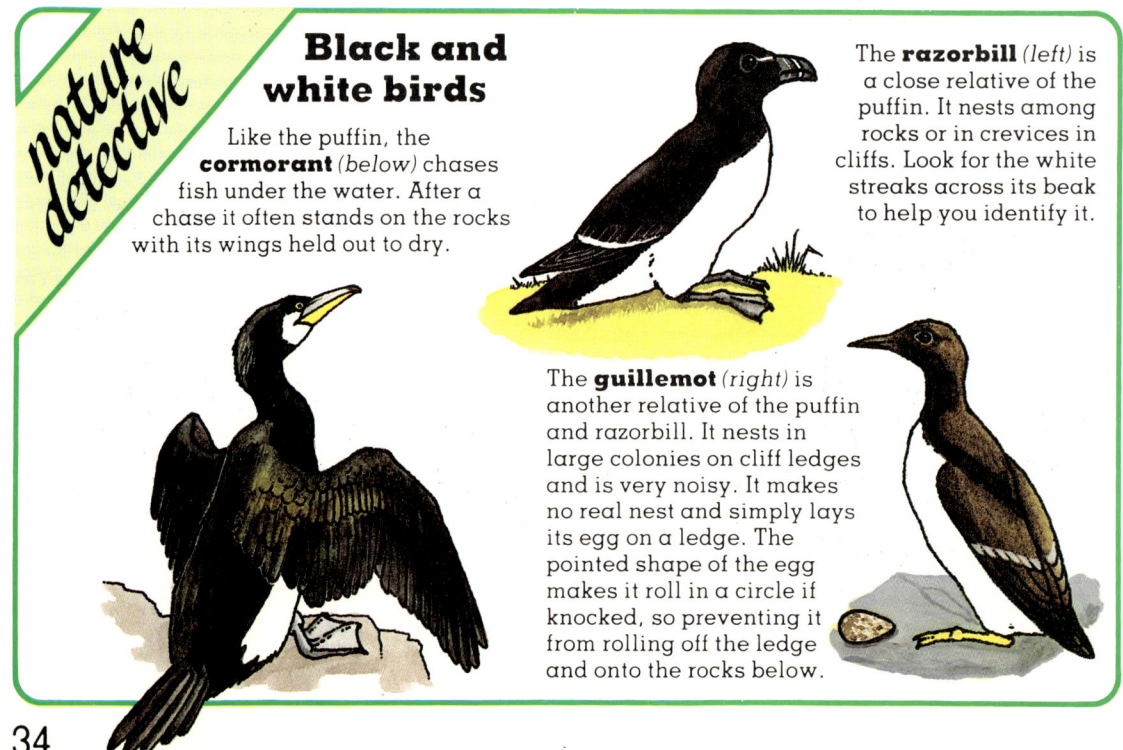

nature detective

Black and white birds

Like the puffin, the **cormorant** (below) chases fish under the water. After a chase it often stands on the rocks with its wings held out to dry.

The **razorbill** (left) is a close relative of the puffin. It nests among rocks or in crevices in cliffs. Look for the white streaks across its beak to help you identify it.

The **guillemot** (right) is another relative of the puffin and razorbill. It nests in large colonies on cliff ledges and is very noisy. It makes no real nest and simply lays its egg on a ledge. The pointed shape of the egg makes it roll in a circle if knocked, so preventing it from rolling off the ledge and onto the rocks below.

Living on the rocks

Most animals have to move about to find their food, but some of the creatures living in the water can actually wait for the water to bring food along to them! And this is one good reason why lots of seaside animals can remain fixed in one place for many years. The mussels in the picture below are a good example of this.

Mussels are often called shellfish because they have hard shells but, despite their name, they have no connection with real fishes. They belong, instead, to the large group of animals called *molluscs* and they are related to the snails. But rather than having a single coiled shell like the snail, the mussel has two shells hinged together along one edge. Each shell is called a valve, and animals with shells like this are called *bivalves*, which simply means two valves.

The mussel is fixed to the rocks by a bunch of tough threads and it cannot move about. However, if it is torn from its moorings it can produce more threads and fix itself in a new place. You can often find lots of mussels packed closely together on the rocks. And if you mark out a 10 cms square in a dense colony and count the number living there, you could find as many as a hundred!

With all these mussels living in one place, you might wonder how they get enough food. This is where living in the sea is a great advantage, for with every incoming tide there arrives a fresh supply of food.

If you watch some mussels in a rock pool, where they are underwater, you will see that their valves are slightly open. They draw in currents of water through the gap and filter out the microscopic plants and other food materials that have been brought to them by the sea.

Sticky limpets

The conical shells of limpets are very common on the rocks. And, if you have ever tried to remove one, you will know that the animals hold on to the surface beneath them very tightly indeed. Limpets are sea snails (although they do not have coiled shells), and they have a very muscular foot which acts like a suction disc to hold them on to the rock. You can see this in the picture below. When the tide is in, the limpets move about and scrape tiny plants from the rocks with their tongues that are just like sandpaper.

Musuclar foot

Crusty barnacles

When the tide goes out on a rocky shore, you might think that some of the rocks in the distance are white in colour. But if you look more closely, you will see that this is due to the little tent-like shells of barnacles. Out of the water, these don't really look like animals at all, and you will probably be surprised to learn that they are related to the crabs. Young barnacles swim freely in the water, just like young crabs, but when they grow up, they settle on the rocks and form white shells around themselves. Try to find a small stone with some barnacles on it. Put the rock in a bowl or bucket of sea water and if you watch carefully, you will see the shells open up as the barnacles start to feed. Feathery legs come out and "comb" the water every second or so, gathering in any small food particles floating by. If you can't find any barnacles on a small rock, try to watch the animals feeding when the tide covers them.

The curious seahorse

Lots of small fish live in the shallow water and among the seaweeds close to the shore. You might be able to catch some of them in a shrimping net or watch them swimming around in rock pools. Several of these seashore fishes have unusual shapes, but none is stranger than the little seahorse. With a head like a horse and a tail like a monkey, it doesn't really look like a fish at all. In fact, the bony ridges all over its body make it look more like a strange wooden carving!

Seahorses grow to about 12 cms long and swim about in an upright position, pushing themselves along by whirring the fan-shaped fin on their backs rather like a propeller. They feed by sucking in tiny animals through their tubular mouths and, when at rest among the seaweeds, the seahorse anchors itself firmly in one place by wrapping its tail around a plant.

The most curious thing about the seahorse is its method of having babies. As with all animals, the female actually produces the eggs, but she lays them in a pouch on the male's belly and it is up to him to look after them after that. He carries them around in his pouch for about five weeks, and during this time the eggs receive both food and oxygen from the father's bloodstream. The eggs eventually hatch and, when the baby seahorses are ready to leave, the pouch opens. By bending and straightening his body with strong, jerking movements, the father pushes the babies out. They are usually born one at a time and after he has given birth to a hundred or more, the poor father is quite exhausted!

The seahorse prefers warm water and is most common around the southern shores of Europe. However, it sometimes visits the south coasts of England and you might be lucky enough to find one lurking in the seaweeds in shallow water at low tide.

The short-nosed seahorse is found only in the Mediterranean. It has a shorter snout and lacks the slender "ribbons" on the body.

Which fish is which?

nature detective

The **butterfish** or **gunnel** (*right*) has a very long fin and 9-13 dark spots along its back. You can find it under stones and seaweeds, and even curled up in empty shells. It grows to 18-24cms long.

Watch out for the **lesser weever fish** (*left*): the spines from the triangular fin on its back are very poisonous and cause a lot of pain if they stick in your feet. This fish spends a lot of time buried just under the surface of the sand in shallow water. So, where it occurs, it is wise to do your paddling in a pair of old plimsolls. It grows to 10-15cms long.

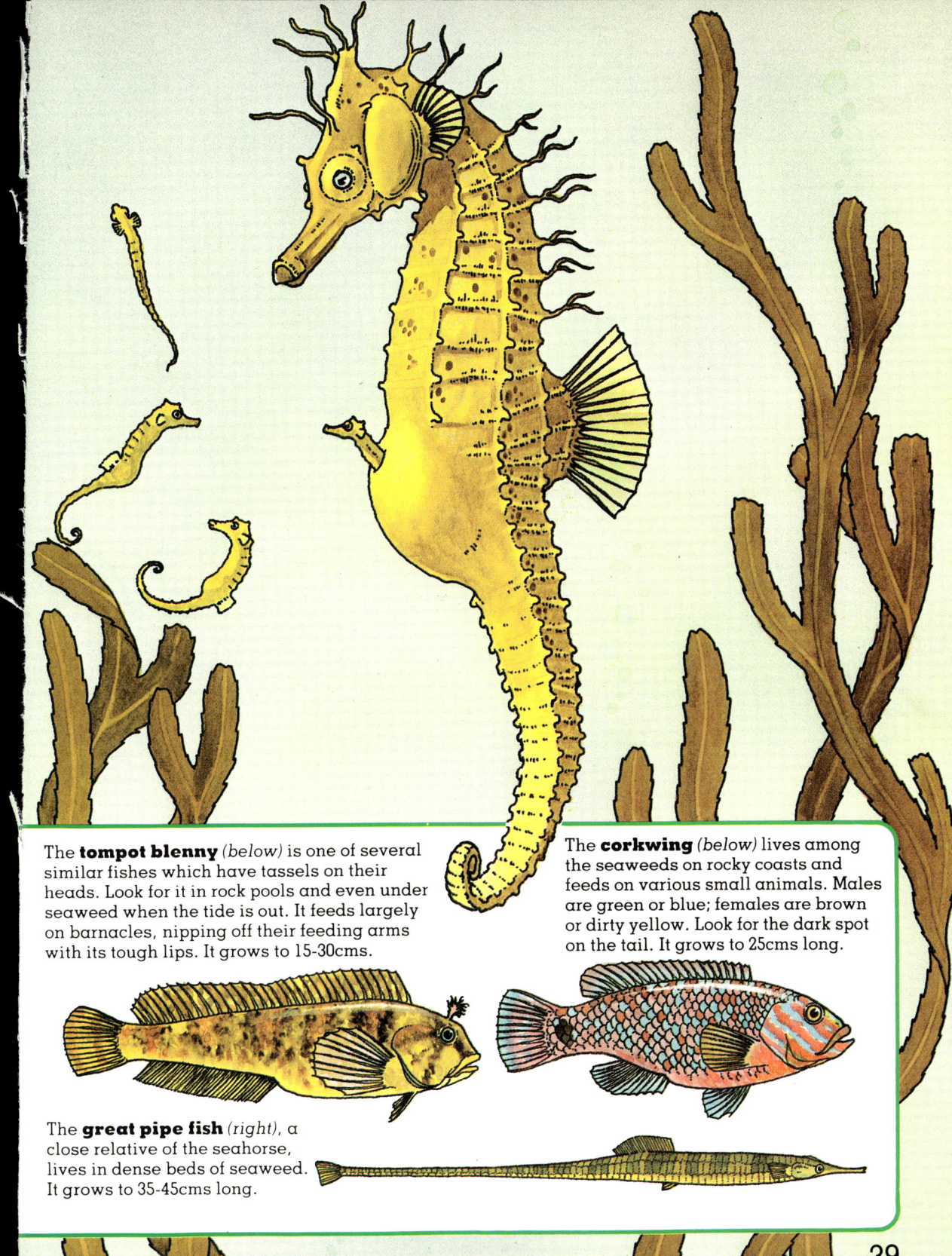

The **tompot blenny** *(below)* is one of several similar fishes which have tassels on their heads. Look for it in rock pools and even under seaweed when the tide is out. It feeds largely on barnacles, nipping off their feeding arms with its tough lips. It grows to 15-30cms.

The **corkwing** *(below)* lives among the seaweeds on rocky coasts and feeds on various small animals. Males are green or blue; females are brown or dirty yellow. Look for the dark spot on the tail. It grows to 25cms long.

The **great pipe fish** *(right)*, a close relative of the seahorse, lives in dense beds of seaweed. It grows to 35-45cms long.

Seaside ducks

The boldly-marked duck in the big picture is a shelduck. It has a longer neck than most ducks, and, unlike many of its other relatives, it remains by the sea throughout the year. Shelducks are not really very fond of water, though, and they never swim very far out to sea. Instead, they spend their time feeding on the various worms and other small animals which they dig from the mud when the tide is out. They can also dabble for food by up-ending in shallow water.

Salt-marshes are among their favourite places, but they can also be found in the damper areas of sand dunes. They make their nests in burrows, often taking over old rabbit holes in the dunes, and the female will lay up to 15 eggs in the nest and sit on them for about a month. The ducklings are taken to the feeding grounds soon after they hatch, and there they meet up with other duckling broods. It is then that a very odd thing happens; for a few adult ducks will remain to watch over the ducklings, while the rest fly off for a "holiday"! Shelducks from the British coast usually fly all the way to Germany, and they lose all their flight feathers when they get there. New feathers grow after about six weeks and then the birds can fly home again.

Many other kinds of duck can also be found at the seaside, but usually only during the winter and along the wilder stretches of coast. They spend the summer months breeding by inland lakes and marshes, but they can't stay there all the year because the shallow waters often freeze in winter and the ducks can't find enough food. They can usually find plenty to eat by the sea, though, because the sea rarely freezes.

nature watch

Flying away for the summer

The bird in this panel is called a **brent goose** and, like many seaside ducks, it comes to Britain only for the winter. As soon as the weather warms up in the spring, the birds all leave for their northern breeding grounds, far up in the Arctic. Use your *Nature Diary* to record when the geese and ducks leave in the spring and when they return in autumn. You may see the geese feeding on plants at the water's edge or flying overhead, sometimes in a V-formation.

Which duck is which?

Use your binoculars to look for ducks along the coastline. How many kinds can you discover living there? Remember that males and females usually have different colours, so you must be careful when identifying them.

The male **eider** is black and white but the female is brown. Both have triangular beaks. They live mainly around northern coasts and feed on molluscs. The very soft feathers from the female's belly have long been used to fill pillows and the eiderdowns that bear their name.

The **long-tailed duck** has a rather short beak but the male has a very long tail. It breeds in the Arctic and comes to British coasts only in the winter. In the summer the male has a black neck and a brown back.

The **velvet scoter** can be distinguished from several similar dark ducks by the white flash on its side. It is another duck that visits Britain only in winter.

Picture index

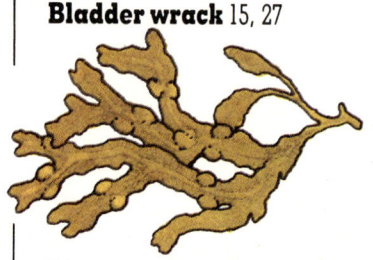